Wetlands

Soggy Habitat

by Laura Purdie Salas   illustrated by Jeff Yesh

Thanks to our advisers for their expertise, research, and advice:

Michael T. Lares, Ph.D., Associate Professor of Biology
University of Mary, Bismarck, North Dakota

Susan Kesselring, M.A., Literacy Educator
Rosemount–Apple Valley–Eagan (Minnesota) School District

PICTURE WINDOW BOOKS
Minneapolis, Minnesota

Editor: Jill Kalz

Designers: Joe Anderson and Hilary Wacholz

Page Production: Angela Kilmer

Art Director: Nathan Gassman

Associate Managing Editor: Christianne Jones

The illustrations in this book were created digitally.

Picture Window Books

5115 Excelsior Boulevard

Suite 232

Minneapolis, MN 55416

877-845-8392

www.picturewindowbooks.com

Printed in the United States of America.

Library of Congress Cataloging-in-Publication Data

Salas, Laura Purdie.

Wetlands : soggy habitat / by Laura Purdie Salas ; illustrated by Jeff Yesh.

p. cm. — (Amazing science)

Includes bibliographical references and index.

ISBN-13: 978-1-4048-3100-1 (library binding)

ISBN-10: 1-4048-3100-2 (library binding)

ISBN-13: 978-1-4048-3474-3 (paperback)

ISBN-10: 1-4048-3474-5 (paperback)

1. Wetlands—Juvenile literature. I. Yesh, Jeff, 1971– II. Title.

QH87.3.S25 2006

578.768—dc22   2006027219

Table of Contents

What Is a Wetland?

What do you call an area of land that is covered with water? A wetland, of course! A wetland is a soggy ecosystem. An ecosystem is all of the living and nonliving things in a certain area. It includes plants, animals, water, soil, weather … everything!

All wetlands have three main things in common: They have water at least part of the year; their soil is very wet; and they're filled with water-loving plants.

FUN FACT

Wetlands are different from many other ecosystems. They do not all have the same kind of weather. Some wetlands are hot all of the time. Others get snow. That's why wetlands can be found all over the world.

can you think of another example of an ecosystem?

Types of Wetlands

Marshes, swamps, and bogs are three common types of wetlands. Each has its own kinds of plants. Grasses and cattails grow in marshes. Shrubs and trees live in swamps. Mosses and evergreen plants grow in bogs. Bogs are made of thick layers of peat. Peat is a spongy soil made of dead plants.

Marsh

Swamp

Bog

FUN FACT

Wetland water can be fresh, salt, or mixed. Inland wetlands have fresh water. Wetlands along the coast have salt water. Wetlands with a mixture of fresh and salt water are called brackish wetlands.

Important Jobs

Wetlands have important jobs to do. They give animals a place to live and raise their young. Wetlands near the seashore reduce storm damage by absorbing the force of strong waves. They also stop erosion. Erosion happens when waves hit the shore and wash away the soil. The roots of wetland plants hold the soil in place.

Other wetlands prevent floods. The ground of a wetland acts like a big sponge. The ground dries out when there is no rain. It soaks up water when there is a lot of rain.

FUN FACT

Fish and other sea animals lay eggs in coastal wetlands.
The wetlands are safer than the rough, open sea. The
wetland water has all the food the babies need.

Water Cleaner

Wetlands are also good cleaners. Water entering a wetland might have dirt and pollution in it. The water slows down as it flows through the wetland. Little pieces of dirt settle down to the ground. The water that exits the wetland is cleaner than the water that entered.

FUN FACT

Farmers often use extra water from nearby wetlands. They water their crops with it or give it to their animals to drink. Because wetlands are such good cleaners, farmers know the water is safe.

Soggy Soil

Soggy wetland soil doesn't have enough oxygen for some plants. Green ash trees, alligator weeds, and other plants have hollow stems or roots. The plants use these stems and roots like straws to suck in more oxygen.

Some wetland soil doesn't have the food that plants need. Plants have to get food other ways. Some plants catch insects. Others don't even root in the soil. Duckweed soaks up food right from the water.

FUN FACT

Bald cypress trees have knobs that stick out of the water near the bottom of the tree. These knobs, called knees, help the tree live. Because there is not enough oxygen in the muddy soil, the knees absorb oxygen from the air.

15

Two Strong Plants

Wetlands are just the right home for some plants.

Two common wetland plants are cattails and water lilies.

Cattails grow on sturdy stems at the water's edge.

Their waving brown seed heads look like cats' tails.

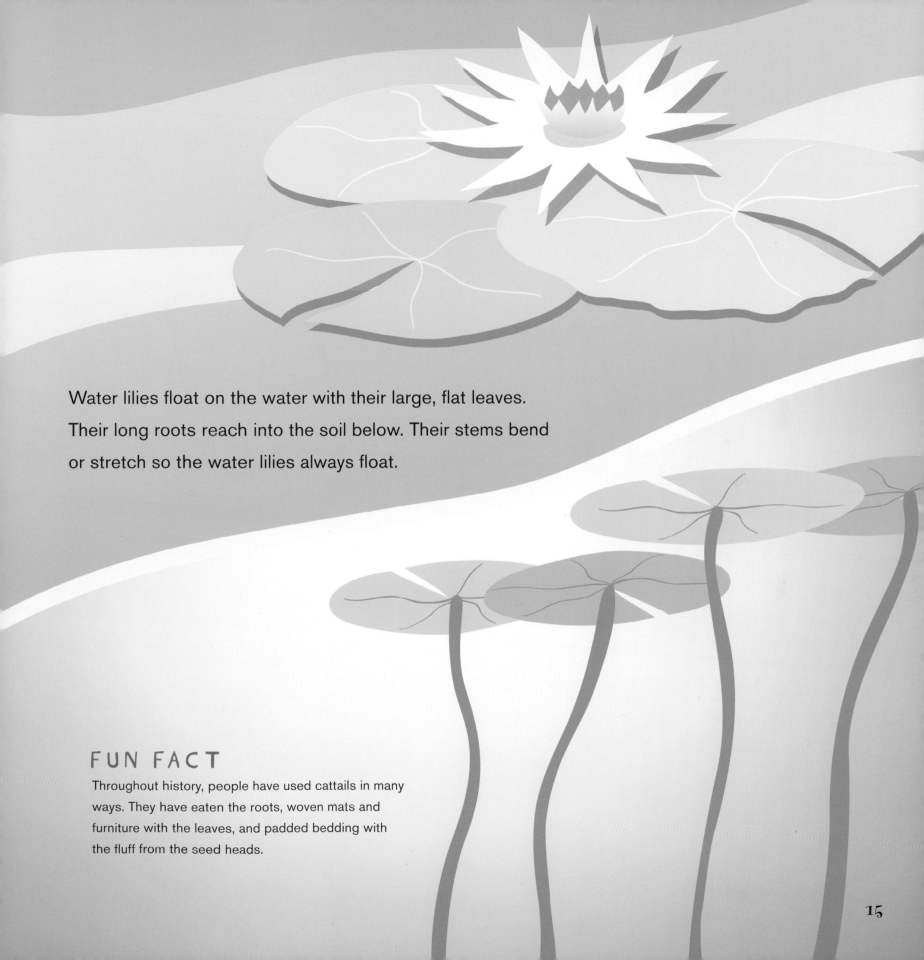

Water lilies float on the water with their large, flat leaves. Their long roots reach into the soil below. Their stems bend or stretch so the water lilies always float.

FUN FACT

Throughout history, people have used cattails in many ways. They have eaten the roots, woven mats and furniture with the leaves, and padded bedding with the fluff from the seed heads.

Wetland Birds

Flamingos, egrets, and many types of ducks live in wetlands all year. They find plenty of fish and other food in this wet ecosystem.

Sandhill cranes and other birds rest or nest in wetlands while they're migrating. More than half of the birds in the United States live at least part of the year in wetlands.

FUN FACT

Egrets, cranes, and herons are all wading birds. Wading birds have long, skinny legs. They wade in the shallow water and look for food. They also have sharp, strong bills to help them catch fish and other small animals.

More Wetland Animals

Birds are not the only wetland animals. Wetlands offer food and homes to many other creatures. Alligators, turtles, snakes, and other reptiles live in wetlands. Mammals such as beavers, rabbits, otters, and deer also live there. So do mosquitoes and other insects. The still water in many wetlands makes a good hatching place for mosquito eggs.

Turtle

Manatee

Alligator

Snake

Beaver

Mosquito

Deer

FUN FACT

Manatees swim in shallow coastal wetlands. These large, peaceful mammals are slow and gentle. Sadly, many manatees are killed every year by boat propellers.

Disappearing Wetlands

Like all ecosystems, wetlands change over time. More or less rain and snow can make wetlands come and go. People can also make wetlands disappear too quickly. All over the world, people drain the water out of wetlands and build houses and farms on the land.

If wetlands disappear, many plants and animals will die. Floods and erosion will happen more often. The water we use for drinking, cooking, and bathing won't be as clean. It's important to protect the wetland ecosystem and all of Earth's other ecosystems, too. Each of them makes this planet an amazing place to live!

FUN FACT

Since the early 1700s, more than half of the wetlands in the United States have disappeared. They have been filled in to make room for the country's growing population.

21

Wetland Diorama: Wetland in a Box

WHAT YOU NEED:

- a shoebox
- a paintbrush
- scissors
- toothpicks

- blue paint
- colored paper
- self-drying modeling clay
- pictures of wetland animals, such as alligators, flamingos, and beavers

WHAT YOU DO:

1. First, turn the shoebox on its side.

2. Paint the inside (sides and top) blue.

3. Cover most of the bottom with blue paper to make water, or try using aluminum foil or plastic wrap. Cover the rest of the bottom with brown paper or modeling clay to make the soggy soil.

4. Use toothpicks and clay to make cattails that stick out of the water. Make paper water lilies. Fill your wetland with animals of all sizes. Toothpicks make great bird legs!

Wetland Facts

- The Everglades is a huge wetland in southern Florida. It is filled with sawgrass and other grasses. Some people call it the "River of Grass."

- Have you ever roasted marshmallows? Then thank a wetland! The people who invented marshmallows used sap from the roots of the marsh mallow plant. The sap made the treat soft and gooey. Today's marshmallows contain gelatin instead of sap.

- Cranberries are grown in bogs. At harvest time, farmers flood the bogs. Then they use a machine to stir the water around. The cranberries come off the vines and float to the surface.

- The water strider is a wetland insect. It looks like a small, light stick with six skinny legs. This tiny bug can actually walk on water! It glides along the surface without sinking.

Glossary

brackish—a mix of salt water and fresh water

ecosystem—an area with certain animals, plants, weather, and land or water features

erosion—when soil is worn away by water or wind

inland—away from the coast

mammals—warm-blooded animals that feed their young milk

migrating—traveling to find food, water, warmer weather, or a place to give birth

oxygen—a gas that all humans, animals, and plants need to live

reptiles—cold-blooded animals with a backbone and scales

To Learn More

AT THE LIBRARY

Galko, Francine. *Wetland Animals*. Chicago: Heinemann Library, 2002.

Kalman, Bobbi. *What Are Wetlands?* New York: Crabtree Publishing, 2002.

Richardson, Adele. *Wetlands*. Mankato, Minn.: Bridgestone Books, 2001.

Sievert, Terri. *Wetland Plants*. Mankato, Minn.: Bridgestone Books, 2005.

ON THE WEB

FactHound offers a safe, fun way to find Web sites related to this book. All of the sites on FactHound have been researched by our staff.

1. Visit *www.facthound.com*
2. Type in this special code: 1404831002
3. Click on the FETCH IT button.

Your trusty FactHound will fetch the best sites for you!

Index

LOOK FOR ALL OF THE BOOKS IN THE AMAZING SCIENCE–ECOSYSTEMS SERIES:

Deserts: Thirsty Wonderlands

Grasslands: Fields of Green and Gold

Oceans: Underwater Worlds

Rain Forests: Gardens of Green

Temperate Deciduous Forests: Lands of Falling Leaves

Wetlands: Soggy Habitat